Tracking a STORM

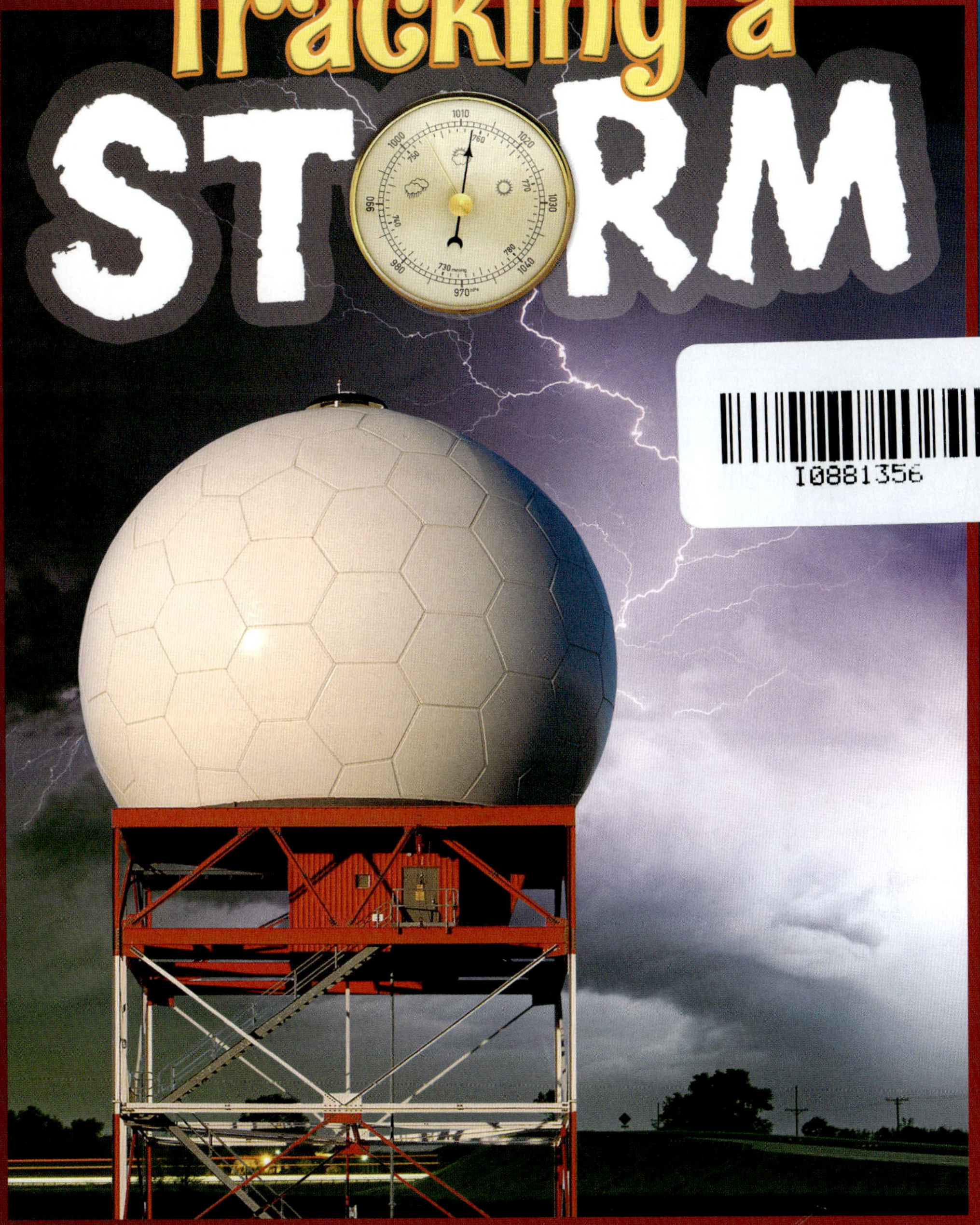

Heather E. Schwartz

Smithsonian

Contributing Author

Heather Schultz, M.A.

Consultants

Kelly V. Chance
Senior Physicist
Smithsonian Astrophysical Observatory

Tamieka Grizzle, Ed.D.
K–5 STEM Lab Instructor
Harmony Leland Elementary School

Stephanie Anastasopoulos, M.Ed.
TOSA, STREAM Integration
Solana Beach School District

Publishing Credits

Rachelle Cracchiolo, M.S.Ed., *Publisher*
Conni Medina, M.A.Ed., *Managing Editor*
Diana Kenney, M.A.Ed., NBCT, *Content Director*
Véronique Bos, *Creative Director*
Robin Erickson, *Art Director*
Seth Rogers, *Editor*
Mindy Duits, *Senior Graphic Designer*
Smithsonian Science Education Center

Image Credits: p.4, p.13 (top) National Oceanic and Atmospheric Administration; p.7 (bottom) National Weather Service; p.11 (bottom) World Meteorological Organization; p.17 (bottom) Chris R. Sharp/Science Source; p.21 (Bottom) Michel Mond/Shutterstock; p.22 FashionStock/Shutterstock; p.23 (top), p.27 (all) © Smithsonian; p.25 (bottom) NASA/JPL-Caltech; p.26 (right) Jim Reed/Science Source; all other images from iStock and/or Shutterstock.

Library of Congress Cataloging-in-Publication Data

Names: Schwartz, Heather E., author.
Title: Tracking a storm / Heather E. Schwartz.
Description: Huntington Beach, CA : Teacher Created Materials, [2018] | Audience: Grades 4 to 6. | Includes index. |
Identifiers: LCCN 2018005462 (print) | LCCN 2018010037 (ebook) | ISBN 9781493869442 (E-book) | ISBN 9781493867042 (pbk.)
Subjects: LCSH: Weather forecasting--Juvenile literature. | Storms--Juvenile literature.
Classification: LCC QC995.43 (ebook) | LCC QC995.43 .S39 2018 (print) | DDC 551.63--dc23
LC record available at https://lccn.loc.gov/2018005462

Smithsonian

Teacher Created Materials

5301 Oceanus Drive
Huntington Beach, CA 92649-1030
www.tcmpub.com

ISBN 978-1-4938-6704-2

Printed by: 70548 Printed in: China PO#: 19435

Table of Contents

Beyond Guesswork

Have you ever been caught in a storm that you did not know was coming? Have you ever dressed in the morning only to have the weather change by lunch? Without a doubt, weather has a huge effect on our lives. We cannot change weather. We can only prepare for it. The more we know about weather before it happens, the better we can plan around it. But weather can be hard to predict and can change quickly.

When you see a weather **forecast**, it is more than just a guess. Modern **meteorologists** (mee-tee-uh-RAH-loh-jihsts) put science to work to predict what the future holds. They can help people plan their day. They can help people decide whether to pack an umbrella. But that's not all they do. They also track tornadoes, hurricanes, and other major storms. They help people plan for disasters—before they strike. Weather forecasts can actually save lives!

The first forecast that predicted a tornado was issued on March 25, 1948. The tornado was headed for Tinker Air Force Base in Oklahoma.

tornado damage at Tinker Air Force Base

damage caused by a tornado

What Is Weather?

When scientists talk about weather, they are describing the state of air at a certain place and time. Many things can affect weather. Air **temperature** is one. Wind speed and **humidity** (hyoo-MIH-dih-tee) can also change the weather.

Air temperature is the most common measurement. People read thermometers to find out the temperature. They help people know how hot or cold it is.

You may have felt humidity before. It can make it hard to breathe. This is due to the **water vapor** in the air. The more water vapor there is, the more humid it is. On a hot day, high humidity makes it feel even hotter. If it is too hot and too humid outside, it can be dangerous.

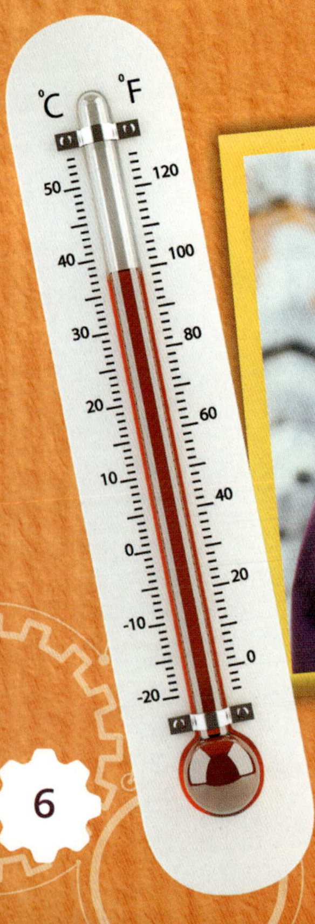

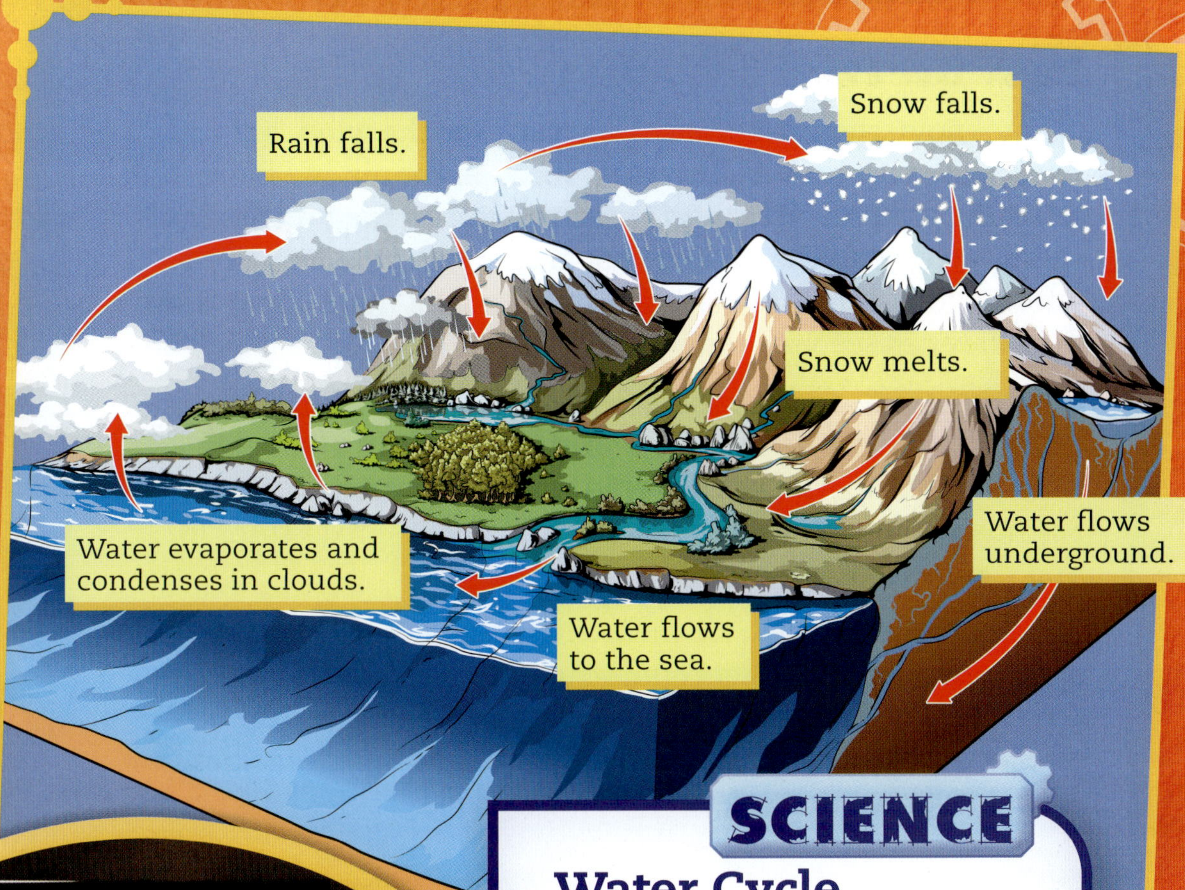

SCIENCE

Water Cycle

In the water cycle, water moves from Earth's surface to the sky and back again. When the sun heats oceans and lakes, some of that water **evaporates**. It becomes a gas, also called water vapor. Later in the cycle, the same water becomes **precipitation**. It falls back to the ground. This pattern has recycled Earth's water for billions of years.

Meteorologists track the weather.

Easy Breezy

You know when it is windy. You can't see the wind, but you can see the effects of it. Leaves fly through the air and blow along the ground. Trees and branches sway in the breeze. But seeing what wind can do does not always give you enough information. Scientists use tools to learn a lot more about wind than they can see with their eyes.

Scientists use anemometers (a-neh-MAH-meh-tuhrz) to measure wind speed. An anemometer is made of a rod with cups attached to it. The cups spin when they catch the wind. Scientists count the number of times an anemometer spins to find the speed of the wind.

A barometer (bah-RAH-meh-tehr) measures the pressure of the **atmosphere**. That is the weight of the air as it is pulled down to Earth by gravity. Atmospheric pressure can help predict the weather. High pressure usually brings clear skies, while low pressure creates clouds and storms.

anemometer

barometer

Air pressure is higher the closer you are to sea level.

Get Your Head in the Clouds

When atmospheric pressure is low, air near the ground rises into the sky. As it moves higher, it cools and the water vapor forms clouds. But anyone who has looked at the sky knows that not all clouds are the same.

Meteorologists watch for different types of clouds to help forecast the weather. Clouds are classified by how high they form as well as by their shapes and colors.

For example, cotton-like clouds that float low to the ground are called cumulus (KYOO-myuh-luhs) clouds. They usually form on a nice sunny day. Cirrus (SIHR-uhs) clouds, on the other hand, look wispy and appear higher in the sky. They are a sign of a coming storm, such as a hurricane. Cumulonimbus (KYOO-myuh-loh-NIHM-bus) clouds are low like cumulus clouds. But they are large, **dense**, and sometimes dark. These are the clouds that cause storms.

cumulus clouds

cirrus clouds

cumulonimbus clouds

By uploading pictures of the sky to the International Cloud Atlas's website, visitors to the site helped add 11 new cloud types in 2017. They were the first new cloud types added in 30 years.

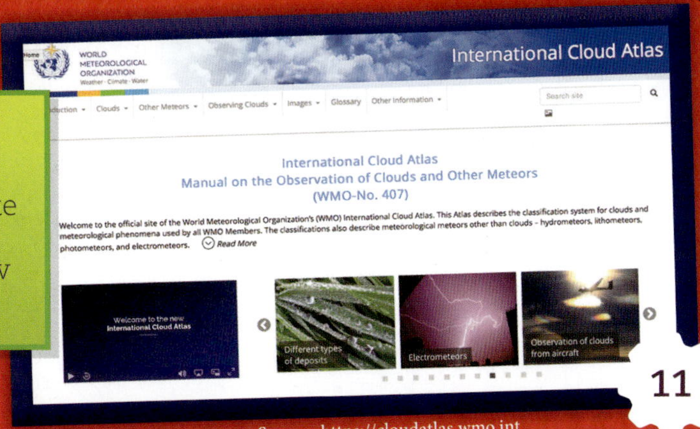

Source: https://cloudatlas.wmo.int

It's Raining, It's Pouring

Precipitation can come in many forms. Rain, sleet, hail, and snow all look different. They feel different, too, if you are outside when a storm hits. But they are all just different ways that water can fall to the ground.

Precipitation is when water vapor in clouds attaches to dust and forms droplets that fall to the ground. Rain is water falling in a liquid state. Hail falls from clouds fully frozen as hard stones made of ice. Like rain, hail can fall in many sizes. Large hailstones can be dangerous. Sleet is rain that freezes in the air before hitting the ground. Many times, sleet is mixed with rain and hail. Snow is made of ice crystals that form in clouds. As they fall, they stick together to create soft snowflakes.

When scientists have enough data about a place's weather, they can determine that place's climate. That is the average weather condition over time.

sleet on the ground

In 2010, a huge hailstone hit South Dakota. It was about the size of a soccer ball and measured 20 centimeters (8 inches) in diameter.

snow over New York City

Watching the Weather

Throughout history, people have used simple methods to see what kind of weather is coming. Many methods are based in science, but they are far from perfect for predicting weather.

An old rhyme states, “Red sky at night, sailor’s delight; red sky in morning, sailors take warning.” It sounds silly, however there is science behind this rhyme.

Weather systems often move from west (where the sun sets) to east (where the sun rises). That means that at night, the sky shows weather on its way. In the morning, it shows conditions that are on their way out.

So, a red sky at night usually indicates high air pressure. Nice weather will follow. When the sky looks red in the morning, however, it means that good weather has passed. There is more water vapor in the air, which means that a storm is likely.

This crystal was used by the Vikings.

TECHNOLOGY

When Vikings sailed a thousand years ago, they used the sun to navigate. It might have been easy to get lost on cloudy days. Modern scientists believe Vikings used an old-fashioned form of technology to stay on course. On cloudy days, they looked at the sky through a crystal. The crystal helped them find the brightest light in the sky. This helped them know where the sun was.

For many years, people have watched animals to predict the weather. Legend has it that cows lie down when it is going to rain. Some people say cows sense the rise in humidity. Others say cows absorb water vapor with their legs. When they absorb too much, they can't stand up anymore.

The truth is, this forecasting method does not stand up to science. When it comes to weather prediction, scientists trust birds more than cows.

Birds have been seen preparing for storms days before they hit. In one study, scientists put small tracking devices on five birds. During **breeding** season, the birds suddenly left their nests, which they normally don't do. The five birds flew at least 1,500 kilometers (900 miles) away. Then, a tornado hit their home. It brought lightning, rain, wind, and hail. After the storm, the birds came back.

The scientists who ran the study believed the birds could sense the storm was coming. Birds can hear **infrasound**, which is a sound that storms make. Humans can't hear infrasound.

ENGINEERING

How can anyone know where a wild bird or animal goes when it is on its own? Scientists developed geologgers to solve this problem. These devices are put on animals and record the time and position of the sun. This data can be used to learn where the animals have been. This process is called solar **geolocation**.

Weather Instruments at Work

It is possible to predict the weather without using any equipment. But meteorologists are more accurate when they use tools meant for the job. Some of these tools are simple. They have been around a long time. You have probably seen and used some of them.

Weather vanes are one example. They have directional markings for north, south, east, and west. An arrow on a rod turns to point in the direction the wind is coming from. One of the first weather vanes sat on top of a tower in Athens, Greece, around 50 BC. It was more than a tool. It was also a decoration. It had the shape of the Greek god Triton.

Even though weather vanes are simple, they are still useful. Keeping a record of wind direction can show patterns in the weather. A change in wind direction can warn that weather will soon change as well.

This weather vane in Prague, Czech Republic, is decorated as a rooster.

ARTS

Modern airports still place wind socks on runways. These long tubes of striped orange and white fabric blow in the breeze to show wind speed and direction. Their colors are more than just decorative. The orange is bright so pilots can see them from a distance. In some designs, each stripe represents a measurement of wind strength.

Rising Waters

A rain gauge is another tool meteorologists use. There are different types of rain gauges. Some are simpler than others. A standard rain gauge catches rain in a 20 cm (8 in.) tube. Markings on the tube show how much rain has fallen.

The tipping bucket rain gauge funnels rainfall into two small buckets. When the first bucket is full, it tips so rain goes into the second bucket. The device measures rain by counting the number of times the gauge switches buckets.

standard rain gauge

A weighing rain gauge collects rain and weighs its **mass**. It can also measure solid precipitation, such as snow and hail.

An optical rain gauge collects rain and uses a light beam to measure how fast it is falling. The beam detects flashes of light in the rain.

This pole measures the height of flood waters.

Hurricane Harvey set a rain gauge record in 2017. Instruments measured between 127 and 152 cm (50 and 60 in.) of rain in Houston over a five to six day period.

Seriously Scientific

Doppler radar is often mentioned in weather reports. This system sends **radio waves**. These waves detect rain, snow, hail, and sleet. The system shows the direction and speed of precipitation. With this data, scientists can tell when storms are on the way.

Scientists also use weather **satellites**. They take pictures and record videos and data about the atmosphere from space. Scientists study these images to track **severe** weather. Then, they warn people about major storms before they hit.

Advance warning about weather gives people time to prepare. They may need to stock up on water and food. They may need to board windows and protect their homes. Or they may need to **evacuate**. Early warning is important when it comes to severe weather. It can save lives.

damage from Hurricane Sandy in 2012

weather satellite

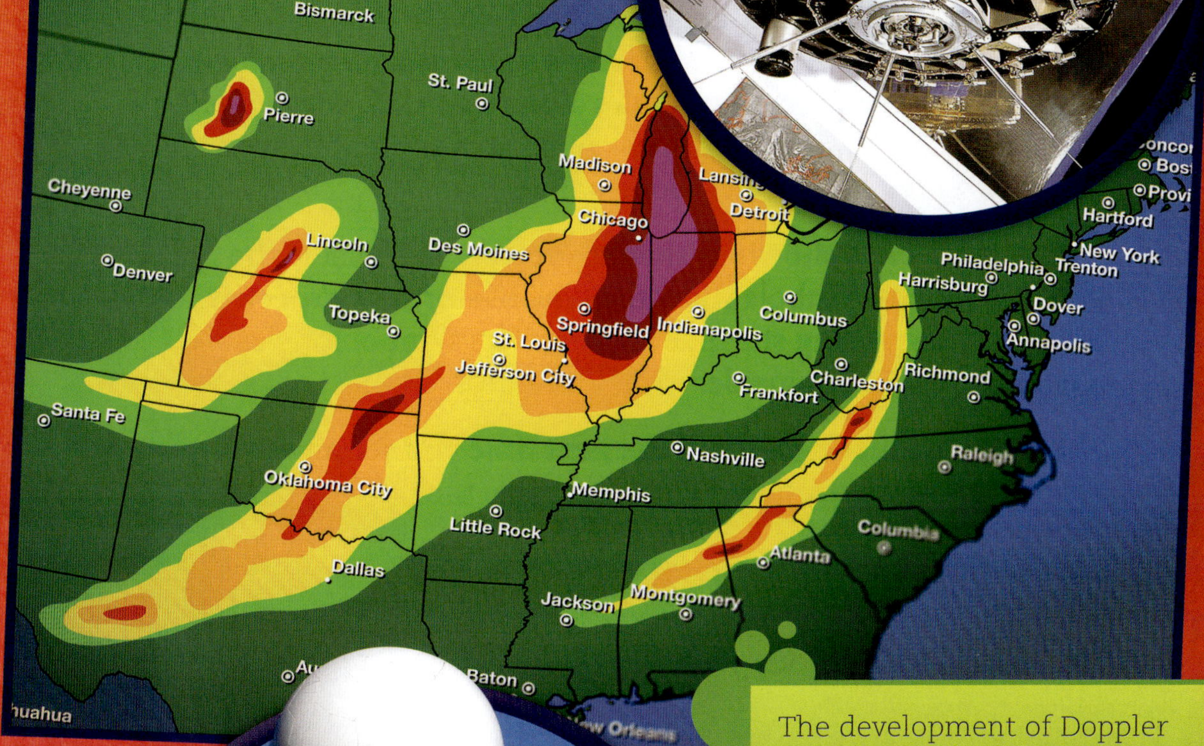

The development of Doppler radar began in the 1940s, when radar technology was used during World War II to detect enemy aircraft.

This round dome protects a Doppler radar antenna from weather.

Data on Display

Data from high-tech instruments and simple tools can be shown using symbols on a surface chart, or weather map. Reading weather maps takes practice. But meteorologists know what each curvy line and sign mean.

A front is an area of change between two **air masses**. A cold front happens when a cooler air mass replaces a warmer air mass. It is shown as blue triangles along a line. A warm front happens when a warmer air mass replaces a cooler air mass. It is shown as red half-circles along a line.

Precipitation is shown as shaded green areas. Inside the green, different symbols show the type of storm to expect. Snow is shown using star-like shapes. The symbol for sleet is a triangle with a dot inside.

Keep these marks in mind the next time you see a weather report. Now, you can read weather maps, too!

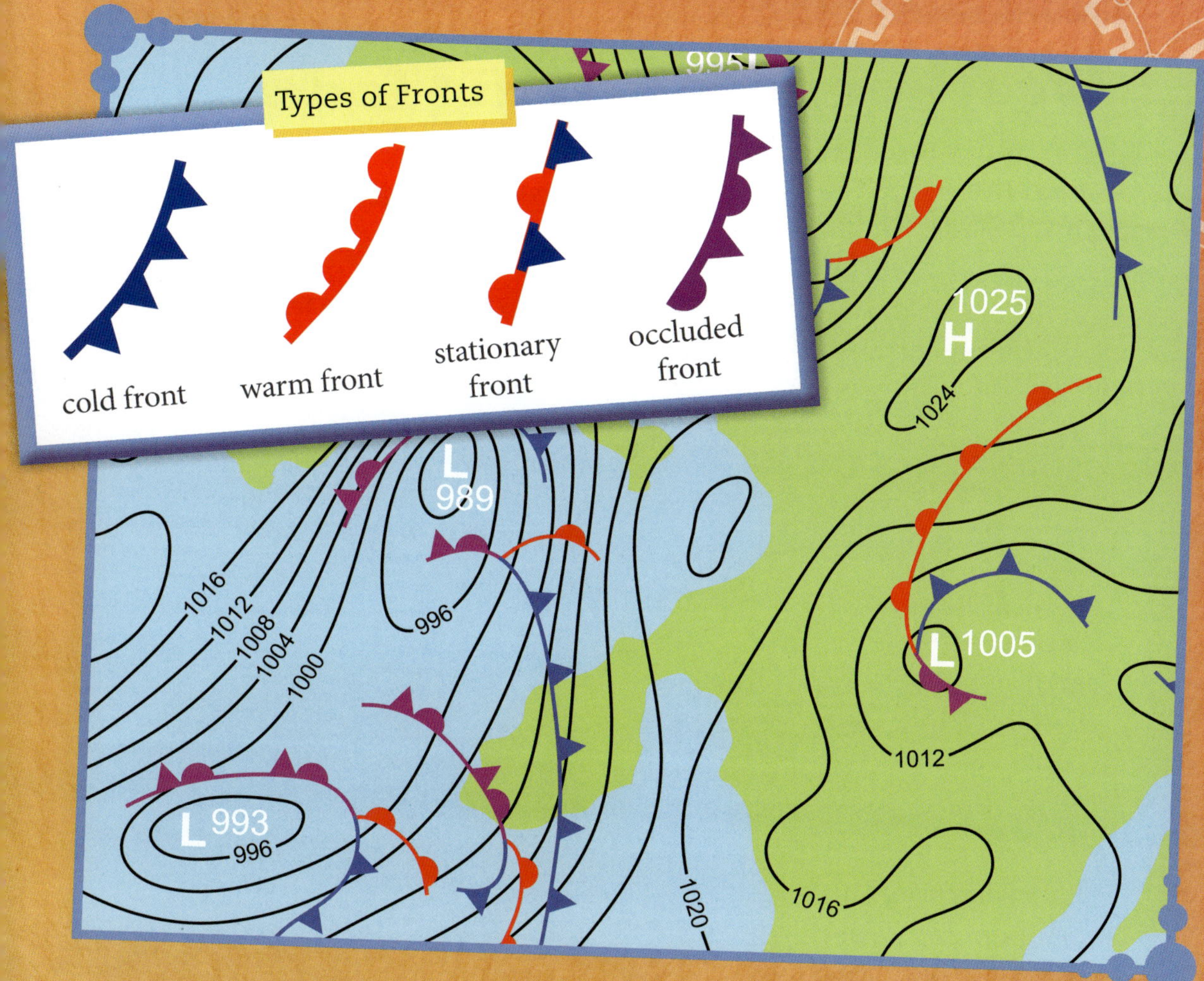

This satellite monitors the environment, glaciers, and flooding.

MATHEMATICS

The National Weather Service is a group that gathers data about weather. It collects data using radar, satellites, and other tools. But what makes the data useful is mathematics! Equations are used to help predict weather up to 16 days before it happens.

Weather Forecasting Today

Weather forecasting has come a long way since the Vikings sailed the seas. They looked up at the sky and only had simple tools.

Now, meteorologists predict weather with many tools. They have data from high-tech weather instruments. They are more accurate than ever.

Meteorologists can tell whether it is going to be sunny or rainy. They can also track severe weather systems. They are the first to know about major storms that can affect our lives.

Extreme weather is dangerous. It can be deadly. But scientists are on the case. They are learning better ways to forecast weather. They are working to develop new tools. In the future, they will spot storms even earlier. They will have even more time to warn people. And they will save even more lives.

TIROS satellite

SEASAT satellite

The Weather Research and Forecasting Innovation Act was signed into law in 2017. It called for more research to improve weather forecasting.

STEAM CHALLENGE

Define the Problem

Imagine your class is creating and installing a set of weather tools to be used at school. Your group has been challenged to design a tool that represents the school and measures wind strength and direction.

Constraints: Your tool must be made out of recycled materials.

Criteria: Your tool must have colors, artwork, and/or symbols that represent the school and clearly show wind speed and direction.

Research and Brainstorm

How is wind strength measured? How does your tool work? Where will it be placed? What materials are used to make your tool? What colors, symbols, or themes represent your school?

Design and Build

Sketch a design for your tool, including any artwork. Build your tool.

Test and Improve

Use a multispeed fan to create different wind strengths. Does your tool clearly show the strength and direction of the wind? Ask teachers and students at your school about how well your artwork represents the school. Modify your design and try again.

Reflect and Share

Does placement of your tool matter? How will your tool be useful to students at your school? Would your tool survive all weather conditions?

Glossary

air masses—bodies of air that have nearly the same conditions of temperature and humidity throughout

atmosphere—the whole mass of air surrounding Earth

breeding—the process by which birds and animals produce their young

dense—containing parts that are close together

evacuate—to leave a dangerous place

evaporates—changes from liquid to gas

forecast—a prediction of something in the future

geolocation—someone's or something's location on a planet

humidity—the amount of moisture in the air

infrasound—sound frequencies too low for humans to hear

mass—the amount of matter in something

meteorologists—scientists who study the weather

precipitation—water that falls to the ground as rain, snow, and other forms

radio waves—energy that sends signals through the air without using wires

satellites—objects in space that orbit much larger objects

severe—very bad, serious, or likely to cause pain or suffering

temperature—a measurement that indicates how cold or warm something is

water vapor—water that is in the form of a gas

Index

CAREER ADVICE
from Smithsonian

Do you want to study weather patterns?
Here are some tips to get you started.

"There are a lot of places that need help tracking storms. Have you heard of Tornado Alley? It is located in the Midwest by Oklahoma and Nebraska. It is famous for tornados. The storms shred homes, destroy farms, and leave people homeless. You can help solve their problem! Can you design a new tool to measure wind speed? Can you build a tool to alert the public before tornadoes hit?"—***Elizabeth Pilger, Production Coordinator***

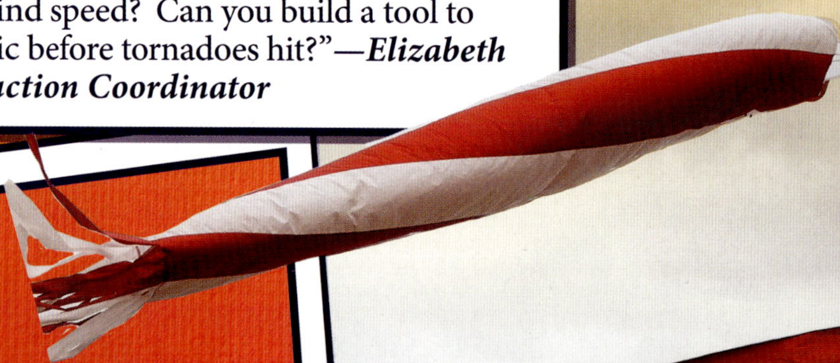

"Build a few weather tools that you can use during different weather systems. A simple rain gauge can give you useful data. A windsock can warn you of weather changes. Try to predict the weather using your tools."— ***Kelly V. Chance, Physicist***